The Usborne

Football
Colouring &
Activity Book

Designed and illustrated by
Candice Whatmore

Additional illustrations by
Lizzie Barber

Edited by
Kirsteen Rogers

Football kit

Use the blank shirt below to design
your very own football shirt.

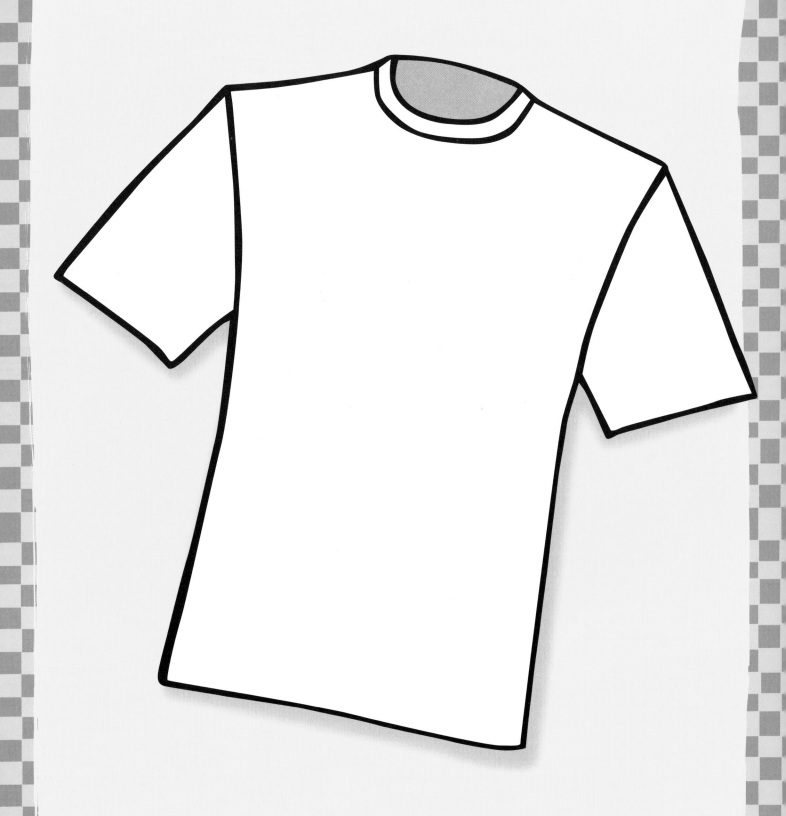

Match-day travel

Football fans journey far and wide to watch their team play. Add faces to the fans in the cars below and draw some more supporters in the coach.

Union City Supporters' Club

Training session

As well as being super fit, footballers need to work hard to perfect their technique. These players are practising different skills. For each one, decide where you think the ball should be, and draw it in.

using the inside of the foot

using the knee

using the head

the heel catch

using the instep (top of the foot)

using the chest

6

Hall of fame

Everyman United's hall of fame is full of photos of its star players, past and present. Add your own footballing heroes to the gallery, by cutting and sticking pictures from magazines or newspapers, or drawing them, in the frames below.

ALEX CLARKE · Goalkeeper of the year · 1982

Club Founder Members
Edward Thomas
Archibald Robinson

Fernando Fereira
Current team captain

Hall of Fame

WAYNE WESTON Top goalscorer 1978

THOMAS ROBSON Captain of Cup-winning team 2009

Alfred Thompson
Football League 1888

Everyman United Football Club · 1907
Players: Archie Advantage (Captain), Bartholomew Boot, Victor Volley, Peter Penalty, Terence Tackle, Wesley Winger,
Frankie Freekick, Ronald Relegation, Harry Hamstring, Bernard Backswing, Morris Midfield, Oscar Offside
Manager: Derek Dribble

Team line-up

The manager has picked his team for today's match. Create your own ideal line-up by cutting footballers' faces from newspapers or magazines and sticking them onto the heads below. Or if you want to, you can draw faces in the spaces to complete your winning side, and colour in the shirts.

Cheering crowd

The fans are having a great time watching their side play.
Design your own banner and flags below to cheer on your team.

RIVERSIDE FC
IS the BEST

Super skills

Write down your dream teams on the manager's clipboard below. Choose carefully – remember you need a range of skills on the football field, not just great goalscorers. You could choose one team of family and friends, and one with football stars.

Manager's Dream Teams

Football stars

Friends and family

1
2
3
4
5
6
7
8
9
10
11

Free kick

These players are practising some fancy footwork. Draw in their legs to match the position of the footballs.

Half-time hunger

Hordes of hungry fans are queuing up for pies and drinks. Cut and stick pictures from magazines or newspapers of things that you'd like to eat to give you energy for shouting and cheering in the second half.

Harry's Hot Food and Drinks

Hot Drinks
Cold Drinks
Burgers
Bacon Bagels
Hot Dogs
Premium Pies
FIZZ
Barbecue Sauce
Tomato Ketchup

Goal!

He shoots. He scores! Draw in the goalkeeper between the posts – it's up to you whether it's a goal or a save. The first one has been done for you.

Foul!

A bad tackle has made front-page news. Make up names of the teams and players to finish off the article below, then add a picture.

SPORTS NEWS TODAY

FOOTBALL PAGES

FOUL PLAY

.... has been stretchered off only thirteen minutes into his début for .... The big money signing had barely touched the ball before he was sent sprawling by a reckless tackle from ....

.... The two-footed lunge earned the .... midfielder a straight red card, but all eyes were on his victim. A spokesman for the club has said the player should be fit for the game against .... in four weeks' time. This news will come as a relief for fans fearing a much longer layoff for their new star striker. The game itself ended in a goalless draw, with no one from either team able to provide the moment of magic that would have broken the deadlock. The man to do it was lying in a hospital bed.

....

Exclusive

NEW DEAL BETTER FOR MILES

Upandcoming City defender Miles Better has put pen to paper on a new contract that will tie him to Beesknees United for the next four years.

The talented midfielder made his international début last month, and has carried on where he left off last season. He set up the winner against Wandering Rovers yesterday with a trademark defence-splitting pass that is fast becoming his calling card.

HUBBLE AT THE DOUBL

Roderigo Hubble continued his fi to the season with a man of th performance against Glebe Co swashbuckling run cut through th defence in the fifty-second m he kept a cool head to slot p Folkes. With ten minutes left o he planted a powerful header post to confirm the win for Con takes his tally for the season to games, and moves his club

Penalty save

There are lots of ways a goalkeeper can stop the ball. Some of them are shown below. For each position, draw in where you think the ball should be.

high shot

punch

body shot

ground shot

palming

diving

24

We are the champions!

It's the end of the season, and Blackbridge United have won the Cup. Fill this page with fizzing fireworks to celebrate.

Trophy cabinet

Design a prizewinner's cup in the space below,
then write the champion's name on the plaque.

The winners!

Congratulations! Your team is top of the table and is this year's league champion. Everyone is clapping and cheering at the victory parade. Finish filling in the league table below, showing your team at the top.

No.	Team name	Colours	No.	Team name	Colours
1.	_____ _____		6.	_____ _____	
2.	_____ _____		7.	_____ _____	
3.	_____ _____		8.	_____ _____	
4.	_____ _____		9.	_____ _____	
5.	_____ _____		10.	Stripes United	

Colouring hints and tips

Use felt-tip pens or coloured pencils to colour in the pictures. Felt-tip pens will give you strong colours, while pencils will have a softer effect.

You could finish this picture to practise colouring.

You can draw patterns within some of the shapes. For example, these football kits are filled with...

...zigzags and stripes...

...checks...

...and diamonds.

Fill in larger areas such as these shorts with lots of lines going in the same direction.

It's a good idea to lay your book on a flat surface while you are colouring, or slip a piece of cardboard under the page you are filling in, to make a firm surface.

If you want to cut out your picture, you'll find a dotted line on each page to cut along.

With thanks to Simon Tudhope.
This edition first published in 2014 by Usborne Publishing Ltd. 83-85 Saffron Hill, London ECIN 8RT, England. Copyright ©2014, 2010 Usborne Publishing Ltd.
The name Usborne and the devices are Trade Marks of Usborne Publishing Ltd. All rights reserved. No part of this publication may
be reproduced, stored in a retrieval system, or transmitted in any form or by any means, electronic, mechanical, photocopying,
recording or otherwise, without the prior permission of the publisher. UKE. Printed in Dongguan, Guangdong, China.